UPGRADE YOURSELF BY UNLEASHING SELF-LOVE
AND DISCOVER YOUR PURPOSE

How Will You Be Listed?

WRITTEN BY

JENNIFER JOHNSON COOK

Copyright © 2020 Jennifer Johnson Cook

All bible verses in this book are from the New King James Version.

ISBN NO. 978-1-943409-72-3

Printed in the United States of America

How Will You Be Listed?

THANK YOU!!!

This book is dedicated to my loving Mother, The Late Mrs. Ruby Wright Johnson formerly of Bishopville SC.
She taught me the principles of being a lady and how to carry myself. Though I got "out of hand" at times she never gave up on me! She would often say "Look like you are going somewhere and stop looking so thrown away" when I would attempt to leave home in my "relaxed look" Those words I detested some days but now, I get it! I'm dedicating this book to you ma! I really wish you were here for me to tell you that all of your fussing, chastising, punishment and your unending love was not in vain! Finally, I GET IT!

My Daddy- Isaac Johnson Sr. He taught me to respect everyone and to never give up when life gets hard! He taught me a lot about life and these things I will never forget! I love you Daddy! I am forever your "Jenny"

To the BEST husband a woman could have, Rodney Reed Cook, I say, THANK YOU! You pushed me, encouraged me then left me

How Will You Be Listed?

in God's hands! I will never forget the look on your face the day I told you that "I'm going to write the book!" you are my covering, my friend, and for that I am thankful!

My kids, Rodneya, Janiyah and Jeremiah THANK YOU ALL!!! The advice, the input, and the missed meals when mommy had to write so that she could complete the assignment! I love y'all!

My Siblings- Elaine, Mary, Jerome and Beverly

Thank you for having a hand in raising me up, I am a product of you! I love y'all!

Table of Contents

What are some of the perks of being properly listed?

How Will You Be Listed?

Intro

Evangelist
Jennifer Johnson Cook

When I was young, I grew up in a small town, Bishopville South Carolina. Within that small town I lived in a neighborhood affectionately known as "The Hill" in a small house. In fact, it was 7 of us in a two-bedroom one-bathroom block home in that neighborhood called "The Hill"! When all of us were home, we had to make that small house work to our advantage and we did! Besides, it was all that we had but it was enough. My father was an outstanding brick mason and my mom was a top of the line domestic worker. They both did excellent

How Will You Be Listed?

work. There were many days I remember seeing my mom come home worn out from cleaning up all day yet, she never complained while standing at the stove on her sometimes-swollen feet to prepare our dinner. She did not just cook hot dogs and fries either (As I sometimes do for my family). No, my momma would cook a delicious full course meal DAILY. The neighborhood would be scented with good cooking every evening because the moms on "The Hill" were all in the kitchen around the same time. I remember a lot about growing up and I am grateful that this rich upbringing played a big part in me being the woman I am today. My father worked in the sweltering heat building structures. He had a job many would not like. He worked that job faithfully and even taught a few of us about the work that goes into brick masonry. Well, I went with him a few times, but I quit after realizing you don't get paid right after the job was done. Don't laugh I was only 7 or 8. My siblings and I grew up in Mt. Hermon Missionary Baptist Church and there all of us had work to do within the church. I don't recall us going out to eat much but we always had food, we didn't go on family vacations, but we did make the best out of being with one another. I want you to get a glimpse of me because we are about to spend some time together, and I want you to know "WHO YOU WIT!" *YOU CAN LAUGH NOW! LOL

I learned a lot growing up. Though I lived a semi sheltered life compared to a lot of people that are my age I learned from where I was. I am a firm believer that I don't have to repeat the mistakes of another person if I only listen to their story. That is why I am here today. No, I do not have any get rich tricks up my sleeves. I am simply here to

How Will You Be Listed?

share my heart with WOMEN! This gives me the opportunity to exercise the demand God gave me back some years ago. **Loving On All Daughters As I Mend For In YOU (Christ Jesus) All Are Healed. YES, LOAD AIM FIYAH!** It's what I heard one morning as I woke up. If I can be transparent, IT SCARED ME BIG!!! It scared me because I knew that it was BIGGER than where I was. I was afraid that I did not have the proper teachings to exemplify such great magnitude. I know how God is about His children and He told me to LOVE ON EM??? At the time I still had short patience and He wanted ME to do WHAT? So, yea, I wrote it down even shared it with a few folks then I decided to put this nice lil cute saying up. I was completely persuaded that this message was not for me! But I was the one confessing that I wanted to help women from all walks of life. From the drug addict to the Corporate

11

How Will You Be Listed?

America worker. That's BIG, and here I am today writing my way into your life. I serve as an assistant that will help you not make the decisions I have made. I do not regret any of them, I just know better now. When you are done you will know better too! I AM SO EXCITED FOR YOU! SO, LETS GO ON A WALK AND LET ME GIVE YOU THE LATEST HOTTEST FRESHEST NEWS!

How Will You Be Listed?

What assignment are you on currently?

How Will You Be Listed?

SALVATION

The BEST thing that happened to me!

I have done a few things in life. I have done some things that I am ashamed of and I've done quite a few things that I am proud of. One of the things that I am forever proud of is the fact that at the tender age of seventeen I made the best choice concerning my soul. I gave my life to the Lord. Yes, I got saved! I was not in a fancy sanctuary; I was not in a booth to confess my sins. No! I was not in the presence of my Pastor; I was simply in my bedroom beside my bed on my knees. Yes, it was just that simple. You may ask why seventeen? That's simple too, I realized that if I did not want to spend eternity in hell I had better repent and turn. I understood fully that the wages of sin were death and the gift of

How Will You Be Listed?

God is eternal life. Either way I was gonna have eternity somewhere and if I wanted it to be in Heaven then SALVATION had better be my choice. I was young and yes, in that short span I had already done some hell eligible things! Before you begin to wonder let me help you. ANYTHING that is not of God is sin. You probably need to repent and turn too. The Bible declares that we ALL have sinned and fallen short, I just acknowledged mine and I shared that with you. It is so sweet to be saved! Life for me got better even with the bumpy roads, stress of measuring up and all that other stuff it got SWEETER. I knew that I had a Father that I could pray to and cast my cares upon. I knew that I had a sure shoulder to lean on and I learned at an early age that I could talk to Him anytime, and I STILL do. Salvation was truly the best listing I have ever had. To be listed SAVED does not mean that I did not ever

How Will You Be Listed?

miss the mark, it means I was forgiven for all the marks I'd miss, and that same grace was readily accessible. Yes, I had friends that weren't yet ready for that walk and a few even said I wouldn't succeed. I believed them because I thought I had to be perfect, I thought I'd always have to get it right and never room for error. Yes, we are to strive for perfection but sometimes we will miss the mark, yes there will be times that we will backslide and find ourselves going the total opposite direction of our goal. Remember sin is sin when we commit such and fail to repent and turn, we then become eligible for hell if in fact we die before we repent and turn. I don't know about anyone else, but I do not like fire. There is nothing about hell that I find appeasing. Are you saved? If so, I am so happy for you. If not let's fix that. Roman 10:9 says it this way," That IF thou shalt confess with thy mouth the Lord Jesus, and

How Will You Be Listed?

shalt believe in thine heart that God hath raised Jesus from the dead, thou shalt be saved. Yes! It is just that easy. There is no fee to be paid it was paid in full before you got here, this is absolutely AWESOME!! Though it is not to be taken lightly, A lot of times Salvation is presented in such a complicated way. Folk try to act like they have the ONLY existing key for the kingdom and in order to obtain it you have to go through them. Not so! If this were so, then the instructions would not have been printed in the Bible. The Bible is also our road map to peace, success, prosperity and wealth. Whatever situation you find yourself in after this point, PICK UP YOUR MAP!

How Will You Be Listed?

How Will You Be Listed?

LIVING AN UPRIGHT LIFE

I will be honest with you, living saved is not easy. I won't tell you that all of your troubles, trials and tribulations will end because they will not, and you will find this to be so. In fact, they are going to intensify! Yep, they're gonna get greater. Why, do I have to endure so much if this thing is paid for already? I'm glad you asked, that is what I wanted to know also, like what in the entire world is happening? Well, here is the facts, satan who was once named Lucifer when he was in Heaven got kicked out because he in his own way attempted to take over! Now you think I'm gonna get to somewhere as nice and lavish as Heaven and try to take over so I can get put out? You are wrong! Welp, that is

How Will You Be Listed?

what happened to Satan, he got stripped of his position, posture. Thus, we know him now no more as Lucifer but Satan. So, I told you he was in Heaven before right and got put out. He does in no way desire that you get the opportunity to enter where he got evicted from. First of all, he is ashamed. Second of all he is envious

so that is why he comes or sends his workers with those evil and deceitful tactics. Sometimes we get entangled in them too. So, living upright is your goal and satan is your distraction, he will come up with all types of situations for us to be tricked so that we will end up on the wrong road. Listen let me tell you a secret, even if this happens and you find yourself on the wrong road just simply turn around. U turns are allowed on this journey, I have made a few. God is so gracious and forgiving. No, I won't use His generosity as

How Will You Be Listed?

weakness either as some do. No! I totally understand that He does not have to bless me the way that He does. He understands that there will be times that we miss the mark this is why He allowed us all GRACE! We live no longer under the law of man whereas if we mess up, we are killed, NO! We are living under grace and God knows I AM GLAD. I can see me now being beheaded for thinking the wrong thing. Yes, to whom much is given much is required meaning, God gives us His Salvation however, there will be a measure that is required by us. We have to work the work of Him who has sent us while it is day for the night is coming when no man can work. So yea it is free we just have to fulfill the rest of the contract and that is working for God. Before you open your mouth to complain consider the fact that we worked faithfully for satan before we got saved. Whenever we are not working for God, we are working for the devil. Being saved helps us to see and accept our purpose. Life is so much sweeter when we get in the area that we were created to be in. Wherever God appoints He also provides so no need to worry about the HOW, He will give you what you need to work the work.

How Will You Be Listed?

Philippians 4:13 I can do all things through Christ which strengthens me!

How Will You Be Listed?

Take a moment and jot down
what this scripture means to you
on the space provided below.
Not just a sentence but elaborate
on the areas that this pertains to.

WHAT IS YOUR PURPOSE? WHY ARE YOU HERE?

HAS GOD LED YOU TO DO ANYTHING lately? Be honest. Are you doing it? If yes, good. If No. Why not? I have a complete understanding that THIS has nothing to do with me! It has everything to do with PURPOSE! I believe that we all have a purpose for which we were created, and it is to be fulfilled before we die. I remember a time when, I had to go out of work due to an issue with my knee. I was a little upset because I did not know how I could have hurt my knee and a hurt knee in my profession (Cosmetology) is a big NO NO! I got frustrated with the doctor because it felt like he was not working fast enough so I took it upon myself to go back to work. I did not tell my husband nor our children I just started

How Will You Be Listed?

back booking clients. Well, that worked a couple of days then the pain returned with a vengeance. It was worse that time than it was the first time and I still did not know why. I politely sat my disobedient self right down. Why would I call myself disobedient? Because when this first began the Lord told me to TRUST HIM! I did, all the way to work. Yea, sometimes I get in my own way. Well, He gets the final word and it was BE SEATED! Unbeknownst to me it was for the releasing of this book- **PURPOSE***!* I sat and began to write, upon doing so I came upon some writings on the same topic from previous years, which tells me I must have avoided **PURPOSE** then too. So, before I go any further, I want to say openly that I repent to God and to you! The treasures that we have in these earthen vessels were created to be used BY God. (Selah) Pause and think about that. In my disobedience I refused to be used

How Will You Be Listed?

of God therefore inadvertently holding some people up from their release. You do understand that your gift brings release to others, right? Your gift(s) is/are needed in the earth. Before you even go any further in this book, I ask that you pause where you are and like me, REPENT for not using the gifting that God has placed in you. Let Him know that you understand that the gift(s) within you is not for you but for those assigned to you. Ask Him where to begin your birthing process of such gifts and then rejoice because you just took a MAJOR step in the right direction! All genders give birth to Spiritual gifts from God. There is no gender in the Spirit! (See Galatians 3:26-29). You are preparing to help somebody! There are so many people that need your gifts and if there ever was a time to release them to the Masses, IT IS NOW!

How Will You Be Listed?

So, you maybe wondering what does any of the before stated things have to be with "How will you be listed?" It has everything to do with it. See when every area of our life is fixed our listing is easy to obtain. God honors order! Have you ever walked in a store and found socks in the deli department? No. If you did would not something be wrong with that? You will notice automatically if you saw something like that because it would be out of place. We are all designed for specific purposes, nobody can do what you were created to do like you! Tell yourself, "I am a Designer's Original! "

Okay, we can begin now! Sit back you have already done a lot. Let me tell you about "Sally"

How Will You Be Listed?

Sally was a beautiful, young, fun loving easy going young lady. She attended church often and was very active in her church. If nobody else came, it was a given that "Sally" would be there and ready to work. The church needs a few more "Sally's" She never sought the "Glory" for the nice deeds that she often did around the church as well as for the many members. Sally remained humble acknowledging that it is God that gives her the strength to do these things. Sally was great at doing the work nobody else wanted to do. You know that work that must be done yet never acknowledged? Even on her jobs she always got stuck with the responsibilities that nobody else wanted. Yes, on EVERY job. It's as if this thing followed her. What her leader loved about her is she carried out these unpopular tasks with not one word of complaint. No, Sally worked each one as a

How Will You Be Listed?

service unto the Lord. Be it at work or at church.

Perhaps, you know Sally. Maybe someone just like her, maybe you work with Sally or attend church with Sally. Maybe you live with Sally or.......... Maybe YOU ARE SALLY! Let's take a closer look.

How Will You Be Listed?

What are some of the responsibilities
expected of you? Go ahead, list them.

How Will You Be Listed?

Notes

How Will You Be Listed?

I KNOW SALLY!

Sally often took on more than she could handle but she did it to keep everyone else from complaining. She stayed late nights at work and at church sometimes only getting 2-3 hours of sleep before she had to get up and start a brand-new day. But she never complained. She would at times be the usher, secretary, greeter and the choir member at church sometimes all in the same Sunday. Nobody ever acknowledged her for this they simply assumed that Sally would always be there. This mentality somehow seeped over into her love life. Sally always got connected with the guys that expected her to always do all the work. Never to be pampered and authentically loved on. Never to show true love to her and much like work and church,

How Will You Be Listed?

they too always assumed that she'd always be there. Do you know Sally?

How many times have you ever dedicated unprecedented time and devotion to someone or something that was in no way deserving? Think about it. Yea, that thing. Yep, he is that one I am talking about. How will you be LISTED?

I am no title chaser by far and I guess I will get the chance to make that clear in my next book, ooops! Did I just say that? Oh well…. Yea that title chasing is not for me. I believe that you ought to witness me doing the work long before I ever get the title. Doing the work without being asked to do the work is beautiful. Stop waiting to be acknowledged for a work that you know you are capable of doing, just simply do the work. The title, if its necessary will come to you verses you chasing it down. If you take your coupons to

How Will You Be Listed?

your favorite super market and after they all have been scanned it does not change the amount that you owe, who would you want to see if the cashier was not able to correct this issue? MANAGEMENT! Right. Why? Because you realize the cashier does not have the proper authority to do what needs to be done in

 order for you to be able to use your coupons. This does not mean the cashier is a bad person in no way they just do not have enough authority to do what you need done. If I need to get a prayer through, I'd call my prayer partner not my dentist. Both are good at what they do, and both are authorized but I don't need a dentist when I want to get in contact with Heaven and release the promises of God.

How Will You Be Listed?

Take a moment to write what is on your heart.

How Will You Be Listed?

HOW WILL YOU BE LISTED?

Come on, let's face it! We all have bitten off more than we were able to chew *so to speak* We have given someone the benefit of the doubt even when we knew we shouldn't have. We have agreed to do the work that no one else was willing to do and later discovered that it was more than we were able to handle. Truth is they waited on us to say we would do it because they knew that we would. We have all

Been a friend to people who were never friends to us. We have entrusted information to so called friends only to find out they were never supposed to be trusted. We have loaned money knowing we'd never get it back. We have all had our back against the wall due to

How Will You Be Listed?

giving someone the benefit of the doubt. WE HAVE ALL BEEN THERE! However, we take complete joy in knowing THAT does not define us IF we learned the lesson and moved forward. You are not what you did! You are not what happened to you! We cannot deny that you did it and we sure cannot negate what happened. What we can do is understand fully that THAT DOES NOT DESCRIBE WHO YOU ARE! (Yes, I was yelling this!)

No, it may not be cashier, manager, dentist or prayer partner but you have a listing and that listing carries weight if you put it on.

Meriam Webster helps me out when I need to know the definition of certain words, let's take a look.

Wife-A female partner in marriage.

How Will You Be Listed?

Fiancée-woman engaged to be married. Girlfriend-a frequent or regular female companion in a romantic or sexual relationship.

We are living in a time when these three terms are used so loosely. Many are referring to themselves as the wife of a man when on paper, this union does not exist. We say I am his fiancée when we know full well that man ain't never proposed to you. Girlfriend is often being used when the truth of the matter is y'all just kicking it, he doesn't even know if a relationship is what he desires. Correct titles help in future planning. Let's park right here for a little while. It is imperative that we know that just because you live with him, cook his meals, wash his clothes, take him to the doctor if he needs to go, listen to him complain about his job does not make you his wife. You are simply doing the job of a wife

How Will You Be Listed?

without the proper paperwork in hand, how sweet of you to devote your life, time, money and effort to this man that has yet to afford you the opportunity to share his last name. All the sex that you have given him was such a nice gesture. How do I know? Because if he has to go to the hospital or God forbids, he dies you will be listed as a "Special Friend, or Fiancée "Well you may say, it doesn't matter to you. Well, it should especially if you have daughters or sons, nieces or nephews. It should matter. I am in no way trying to talk down to you, I simply want you to get and have what belongs to you and that is RESPECT! You are a "Designer's Original" do not forget this. See we are teaching life lessons by our life living. If for nobody else, we ought to want to be right in the eyesight of God. In order to receive the blessings of God we have to walk upright before him. I ought not want a title in the church when I

How Will You Be Listed?

don't have one at home. How is it that we have Giants in the church that their families are unaware of at home? Remember we talked about doing the work before the title? This is one of those instances. Charity begins at home. That is the whole problem, we want to be the Archbishop at Church and a "Special Friend" at home. This has got to be fixed. I am in no way saying go get married tomorrow but put the conversation on the table. Maybe he doesn't want to be married, that is something that you deserve to know. Please understand none of what you just read was written in a harsh or fussing tone. Look at it as a full-length mirror, it will help you if you use it.

Fiancée is not being engaged to someone for 10 years and granting them full access to your body, soul and mind without a date of solidity. You need to know what the plan is

How Will You Be Listed?

to make this thing solid. Of course, this is done after all the other prerequisites are taken care of. Yes, you gave me this ring and it is still as cute as it was the day you gave it to me but, what is the plan? No man should have this much access without a plan to make it official. He, my friend is getting the milk without the trouble of buying the cow. I am in no way bashing men. I have a son and it is my prayer that he would love her the way God intended for her to be loved. I am hard on him as it pertains to females simply because I want him to have a healthy respect for females. Ladies understand this, we are the highway that brings life into the world, don't you consider yourself special? A man cannot do that.

Girlfriend? That is okay for a season but just like your nice cell phone pretty soon you ought to be on the upgrade list. The reasoning

How Will You Be Listed?

behind the upgrading of your phone is so that it can operate effectively for the time that you are in. You ought not be his girlfriend after 2 years. That is a long time to just give someone your time in hopes that it will grow to something more. If you go to your job and after 2 weeks you don't get a paycheck would you say something? Why? Because you have put in the work now you want the reward of those benefits, right? Well, my love…….. That is what I am trying to tell you. You deserve it so why don't you have it? Do not rush into anything but you deserve to know which way the both of you are headed.

Shall we talk a little more? Okay, next page.

How Will You Be Listed?

I know that it is never a good idea to get married when you know that you are not ready to become a wife, I get that, and I totally agree. I am also aware that before we can genuinely love someone, we must first, and foremost love God and we must love ourselves. Face it, what can you do apart from God? Whether you think it is important or not it helps a whole lot when the two of you are loving the SAME GOD! Also, if you do not love yourself how are you expecting him to? You must know beyond a shadow of doubt that if everybody walks away YOU are going to be there for yourself. Love God, love you, Know you and Value your worth. Whew…. that is a lot, right? Good because good men love work. Can you imagine here is this guy and he has himself together and he approaches this woman that loves God, loves herself, she is full well able to enjoy a meal alone and she knows her worth, he won't tell

How Will You Be Listed?

you but he just got the ladder out for this tall order. Stick with me, we are going somewhere! Text them back later, we have to finish this!

Let's go shopping.......

Sally went to a yard sale (you thought I was done with her didn't you?) and while at this yard sale since she is an avid money saver, she was able to negotiate the pricing on everything that she wanted. She later visited a super center that allowed price matching, so she took all the local grocery stores ads in that store and price matched all the items that she wanted. Boy was Sally rejoicing over the Money that she saved. But when Sally went into the Department Store it was not like the yard sale nor was it like that super center. She found a pair of pants that had a spot on them, and they weren't even willing to bring the

How Will You Be Listed?

price down at all. They told her that she could put them back if she was no longer interested. As it pertains to dating which are you? Are you allowing him to set the standard by which you will be listed as with the yard sale? Are you allowing him to tell you what his last girlfriend did and cause you to price match like the supermarkets or are you like the department store that has all their pricing set and NON-NEGOTIABLE? As practical as this may seem it is as real as can be. As I said before "Men prefer to work for it" Does this mean he won't take advantage of an "EASY" opportunity? No ma'am he surely will but that WORK, he won't ever forget. After you get your paycheck, why do you spend your money

slow? You spend your money slow because you worked hard to get it. The same is so with dating and in relationships. You value what you had to work for, you take care of it differently when there is a price that you had to pay for it.

Momma said this to me, and I have not forgotten it since, "A man will never buy MILK when he has a COW in the back yard!" I thought those were the absolute harshest yet mildly confusing words she could ever say to me. Then I gave it some thought, Men like work. Who buys milk when a cow GIVES MILK FREELY so, as long as the cow is giving milk why not drink? This does not mean he lacks the money to purchase milk, there is just not a need to do so. We tend to be too much too soon for men then we are upset when he goes and marries the complete opposite of who we were to him. After a few failed relationships filled with lies, broken promises, promiscuity, cheating, and a whole lot of drama I knew exactly what I did not want in a relationship! For a season I even

How Will You Be Listed?

thought that I would never enter another relationship. I was simply tired…... It was later that I learned I was doing this thing backwards, yes I learned that I needed to be able to love me, how could I expect for someone who barely knew me to love me when I knew myself all of my life and yet I did not love me the way that I should have. I had to learn how to enjoy my own company, as a result I began being alright with enjoying me, loving me, taking care of me, doing nice things just for me. Understand I was not doing these things selfishly, but they were all just for me. I learned to take myself on dates before I expected it from a man. I learned the value of SELF WORTH! I learned that after loving God I was next. I am here to tell you that even though I had to go through pain to get to this place I was alright when I got there. When that life lesson sunk in, I was as lethal as any weapon you could purchase. I began

How Will You Be Listed?

to enjoy my company and make **ME** a priority and it felt great! Afterall I was most deserving of it. I enjoyed my company so much til I almost missed the husband I had prayed so fervently for. I literally watched on as I transitioned from the "Yard Sale" Jennifer to that """ Super Center version" and eventually into this "Department Store Woman" that I learned to love dearly. You ask, who taught me? LIFE! Life has many classes for us if we take the time to learn the lessons each class has to offer. I learned some of my most productive yet costly lessons from LIFE! That is what got me here to this very point: LIFE!

How Will You Be Listed?

What is your purpose? Why are you here?
After you have meditated on this question
     write below

The answer (s) that are revealed.

How Will You Be Listed?

HOW DEEP IS YOUR LOVE, FOR YOU?

Do you love you? Do you enjoy your own company? When is the last time that you took **YOU** on a date? How deep is your love for you? Do you compliment you? How often do you encourage yourself? In order to receive the love of a man you must work on the homework listed above. When we don't love ourselves, we tend to be insecure believing that someone else will always do things better than us, they will get the job before us, they will go on the date and not us. Everything good will always happen for them but not us. At least that is what we think anyway. They will get the proposal party, gender reveal and baby shower before we even experience real love. We will tend to self-sabotage

How Will You Be Listed?

'Dumb me" "I'm so careless" "I am stupid"
You have got to love you more or nobody
will. If this is, you I beg of you to make this
the last time you said these ugly things about
yourself the LAST time ever! You are
somebody and YOU MATTER! When I
began to expect more than being a secret, I
received just what I expected. I prayed for
more and I got just that after I began to value
who God created, ME! Right here I want you
to do a self examination be honest. I want you
to see how deep is your love for you. I don't
care how you are currently listed, check the
love that you have for you. Whenever I need
clarity of a word, I look it up. The definition
of love according to Meriam Webster is: 1: a
quality or feeling of strong or constant
affection for and dedication to another. Get
some paper and a pen. Write down what you
are good at, then congratulate yourself, YOU
MATTER! Now write out your weaknesses

How Will You Be Listed?

and beside each weakness write a plan of action to fix this if its counseling, dr visit, forgiving someone that hurt you. Make a goal to correct every weakness that you are capable of correcting what you cannot fix leave it to God and when you complete it date it and celebrate your win! I am already proud of you because things are about to get easier yes just that easy! Write what you can and will no longer deal with. Anything that disrespects or defile you needs to be fixed.

How Will You Be Listed?

What I LOVE ABOUT ME!

(HOW deep is your love for you?)

THIS ONE I CANNOT HELP YOU WITH-
LIST EVERYTHING THAT YOU LOVE
ABOUT YOU HERE BE KIND TO
YOURSELF AND WRITE IT OUT
HONEY!

How Will You Be Listed?

DO NOT BE AFRAID TO LOVE "AGAIN"

I HEAR YOU! You are saying you have tried all of that before and it did not work. You gave it your all, you offered all that you knew to offer you assisted with his goals and dreams and all it did was explode in your face and left you in scraps. Can I share something with you? Some of the best quilts I have ever used were created from scraps. Do not discount your scraps because they were the result of

brokenness. I know what relationship hurt does. Sometimes it leaves us bitter and refusing to trust or love again. That is why I entitled this do not be afraid to love again.

How Will You Be Listed?

Sometimes we fall in love with an idea and end up getting hurt as a result. Baby that was the best thing that could have happened. Because that is one thing you now know not to do. Pray and ask God to give you insight and wisdom as it pertains to what is next. But whatever you do DO NOT GIVE UP ON LOVE! I don't care how old you are or how hurt you are there is hope. This time do it God's way. He is the only one that knows the plans for our whole life. We as women love hard and some of us love fast, that is in our makeup that is the way we were created we are nurturers don't change who you were created to be because someone did not appreciate and value the worth of it all. There will be a man that will come along and both value and appreciate who God created you to be and his only question will be "Where have you been all of my life?" You may say yea right, this won't ever happen for me. To you

How Will You Be Listed?

I say, "We have what we say" This is all according to your faith. If you don't desire it then keep speaking negative and you will always get a negative response. You must have faith and BELIEVE!!!! Believe that God has the final say and He is the keeper of your soul. We must believe that every relationship is not quarrelsome, bitter, draining, and bloodthirsty. No there are some healthy relationships out here. I cannot tell you that you will be in a better relationship by this time tomorrow, I am not certified to assure you that once you are done with this book everything will fall in place. What I can promise you is this- There is no failure in God.

How Will You Be Listed?

How Will You Be Listed?

Notes

I PRAYED AND WAITED AND WAITED AND PRAYED!

After all that loving on me and enjoying my own company and doing my own thing, I realized that I also desired the love of a real man that valued me as much or more than I did. Maybe there were dating sites then, but I went to the Master of ALL – Jesus. I prayed and verbally declared what I wanted in a man, but nothing happened until I wrote it down.

There I was, riding down the road talking to my husband out loud in my car, at least that is what I called it. The Bible declares that we are to call things that are not as though they were. Therefore, I left a seat for my husband whenever I went to church, yes, on the end. I

How Will You Be Listed?

would go to the inner side of the seat and leave the end seat open for my husband. If someone came and desired to sit on that row, I would politely lead them to sit on the other side of me. I'd have my Bible positioned in my husband's seat and somehow, I never had to tell a lie to say "Someone is sitting here" I guess it was God. Girl, I went as far as planning an entire wedding, bridal party and all. I went looking for bridesmaids' dresses too. I was even so sure that this was going to happen that I began to tell folks I was getting married. That was the laugh of many of their days. I would assure them it was true by calling off my bridal party. Once calling off all of them they would all ask the same question, "Who is going to marry your crazy self?" I'd respond by saying "That is the only thing I'm missing, a groom!" I was always good at making people laugh even if I was not trying to. I guess they chopped this up as

How Will You Be Listed?

another one of those times- UNTIL I GOT
MARRIED THE NEXT YEAR!

Yes. I spoke it and I declared it and God was
making my husband even then. I will be
honest and say, many days it felt just like my
time would never come but, It DID! God
knew I was of a different breed and would
require a husband that was okay with that.
Yes, when I was declaring it, I had no clue of
who he was. It took a couple months for me
to realize he was everything I wrote and
asked God for plus more, because God does
not "HALF DO" ANYTHING! Neither one
of us are perfect I am sure that I get on his
reserve nerve frequently, but we make it
through.

How Will You Be Listed?

- John 14:13 And whatsoever ye shall ask in my name, that will I do. That the father may be glorified in the son!

How Will You Be Listed?

THE WORK OF THE WAIT!

I Understood fully that I wanted to be listed as a "Wife" I knew that full well but, I still had to wait and rejoice with others as they dated, and I had nobody to date. I had to be happy and attend weddings alone. I knew that I did not want to be engaged for a long period of time, I knew I did not want to date long, and I was sure that I NO LONGER DESIRED to be a man's secret. I did not always feel this way but at that point I was never so sure about a thing. Yes, this church going girl didn't always believe she deserved a husband. Nope! It was not until I fell in love with ME that I wanted more for me. I realized I no longer had to settle for the lesser. Because the Bible tells me I can have

How Will You Be Listed?

whatsoever I say. That let me know that I was NOBODY'S part time love. So, I waited on my vision to come to pass! It tarried but when it spoke, IT DID NOT LIE! I sung in more weddings during that time then I ever had. I had to wait and be of good courage and God surely gave me the very desires of my heart. I was even asked during my waiting season to go shopping for my cousin a wedding gown. I felt sure that was a trick. Why me? I did it at first, but my heart was not in it. She asked could I go back the next day because she had to work, reluctantly I did. The Lord spoke as I was looking and said "Look as if its your dress that you are seeking for." So, I got lost in wedding attire and I loved it, guess what? I found her dress and she loved it. None of that made sense to me until I wore it the very next year in my wedding. Yes, in finding my cousin's wedding gown I found

How Will You Be Listed?

my own. It reminds me of the scripture that tells us that we reap what we sow.

By the way…... what does that say to you?

How Will You Be Listed?

He Found Me.................

**PROVERBS 18:22 He who finds a wife finds a good thing,
And obtains favor from the Lord.**

Yes! I was nervous, yes people were saying don't do it, its too soon. They also told him I wasn't the "Church Girl" that I was posing to be. They told me that he was not done with the streets yet. Somehow the voice of God always rung louder than the noise of the naysayers. We felt confident that we could trust the leading of God. Yes, we had questions seeing as how we did not have the typical 5 years of relationship. Let me give you the timeline:

How Will You Be Listed?

Started Dating-August 1997 (neither of us remember the exact date)

Engaged- December 19th, 1997

Married- May 16th, 1998

No calculations are necessary, that is 9 months honey! Nope, I was not pregnant, HE JUST FOUND ME!

But I knew what I did not want and that taught me what I did want. I had my revised standards in place, and it was no secret what I would and would not deal with. He knew what he wanted in a woman and what he did not want and behold HE FOUND ME! One of the biggest things I recall him saying was he wanted to rekindle his relationship with God, and he needed my help to do that. If I knew nothing else, I knew all about getting a connection established with JESUS CHRIST. He needed Jesus and I had Jesus yet needed to learn how to love again. Though I was

How Will You Be Listed?

expecting a husband I realized a part of me still needed to heal so we traded! Broken relationships from times past had left me bitter in some areas. Dealing with the stress of broken relationship long enough can leave you damaged. But I am so glad that damaged and all I MADE IT and I did not go on the mark down shelf! I remember when I was ashamed to admit this, but it is very true. I was sort of like a broken ceramic pot, it no longer obtains the ability to hold anything but that is the reason it was created. So, here I was back on the Potter's wheel being made over. I obtained value, just needed to be put back together, and allowed the time for my process to complete. I hope that makes sense.

How Will You Be Listed?

How Will You Be Listed?

Notes

MARRIAGE, ARE YOU READY FOR IT?

Marriage is WORK! I will not be the one to say to you that everyday will be as beautiful as that pricey wedding that you are desiring. There were days I would ask myself, "Did I answer all of the questions correctly in my vows to make us officially married!? LOL!!! After our first two weeks I went back home to my momma. It was not because he was a bad husband, he was doing the very best that he could. I will explain it like my momma and my momma in love explained it to me- He was his momma's baby and I was my momma's baby we were both used to having our own way now we were forced to find OUR way and that was a challenge. Not to

How Will You Be Listed?

mention me being only 20 years old, if I wanted a drink I couldn't even buy it yet (No, I do not drink, but if I did!)LOL! There I was signing a contract with a man that I had only known for 9 months to be with the rest of my life and share a bed with him, kitchen, bathroom, and everything else. It was overwhelming. Yep, I realized that marriage was not just a whole lot of SEX it was even more WORK! NEVERTHELESS. I am still not sure if our moms talked but I asked my mom could I come home and she said no, go pray! I then asked his mom could he come back home she said no, pray! Those were some bitter words to swallow when I truly did not want to hear them at all. But I now realize that those words were

 better than any gift that they ever gave us, for this I am GRATEFUL! Marriage is work; it is not to be entered into unadvisedly.

How Will You Be Listed?

How Will You Be Listed?

YOU WERE NOT CREATED TO BE ABUSED!

DOMESTIC VIOLENCE IS NOT OKAY!

So many women and men are being taken advantage of by their spouse. This is never right. Understand that abuse can be both physical and verbal. There is no person that has ever been created that has the God given right to abuse you. I had to address this because it is all a part of being "Listed." Abuse ought not ever be a part of our listing. If by chance a man feels the need to express his anger through physically abusing you then you ought to be seeking professional help. No ifs ands or buts about it. YOU DESERVE MORE! Yes, he maybe going through a phase, he maybe in a tough time right now, things may have taken a dip for him. None of these excuses him for putting his hands on you. Yes, he may get it together later but while he goes to counseling you take cover. You were not sent to train him by way of abuse. Besides, what are you teaching your daughters? What are you teaching your nieces or the little girls and young ladies in your church or social group? What about the women that see your scars? You are a walking billboard and believe it or not you teach more lessons silently than you are aware of. Even more so than that, YOU MATTER! I can tell you this because I used to think that if a man does not hit you it was because he did not love you. Yes, me! So, I dealt with it because I thought that was love.

How Will You Be Listed?

I thought that it was love to be disrespected by your boyfriend. It was a norm for him to "Degrade" me in front of his homies. Yes, my name is Evangelist Jennifer Johnson Cook and I once thought abuse was okay. It got to the point that I expected it and if it didn't show up, I thought the guy was weak. You may laugh but you will also be amazed of the females that feel the exact same way. I am here to tell you IT IS NOT OKAY. For me it all happened in my earlier years. Sad part is it had to keep happening in order for me to see the horrendous cycle. My way of thinking was premarital sex was the only way to keep a man cause 'Don't no man want no virgin." Yes, that is what I thought and guess what, if not you then some female in your lineup thought or is thinking the exact same. That is why you are reading this book Boo! Thank Ya Now! Denial is a beast that has a tendency of holding us all captive and

How Will You Be Listed?

I WANT YOU FREE! I have never seen a butterfly survive in a jar. I have never seen flowers grow in dry places. The enemy desires to see you in bondage and deprived but, after you are done reading this book you will only travel the roads that lead you to freedom! Freedom from abuse of any type because none of it is permissible! It is my desire that you fully understand the value that you carry. I want you to know that when God made you, He meant to do it! You were not created with black rings around your eyes! You did not come here to be cussed out and talked down to! No, you are here on a divine assignment and you must do it.

How Will You Be Listed?

How Will You Be Listed?

How Will You Be Listed?

It's What I Want

Before you were even created in your mother's womb, God loved you. John 3:16 tells us "For God so loved the world that He gave His only begotten son that WHOSOEVER BELIEVE in Him will not perish but have everlasting life. He loved us before we got here, and He gave His ONLY son as a ransom for us. You know how you see that nice bag, or those bad shoes and you come to the conclusion that you want them? You don't want them because they have no potential, no, you want them because you know the outfits that you already have that these items will accent well. So, you begin to

How Will You Be Listed?

figure in your head how can you save your money up so you can in fact purchase them, right? Well, before God saw us, He went ahead and made an advance payment for us, because ANYTHING HE MAKES IS GOOD! He knew that we were what He wanted, and He did not mind paying the price, even if it was all He had. My God!!! Well, guess what? When a man meets you or if he hears street chatter of you before he officially meets you, he already has a preconceived idea of his plans for you. Yep! Let me tell you what confirms it for him, your posture! The way in which you carry yourself is what confirms or cancels his plans. If you meet him and your standards are high and you are well kept before y'all begin to date, he already knows that he has a standard to meet if he is going to be with you. When you open your mouth and speak with dignity and respect, he already knows what is up and if

How Will You Be Listed?

his plan was otherwise, you probably will not ever see him again. But you can be that same well-kept good-looking lady yet disrespectful as it pertains to yourself, he will in fact follow suit. When its what he wants he will work for it. I am not referring to sex, I am talking about your time, intellect and your attention. He will do what must be done to obtain what he so desires. Just like God giving all He had and you saving that money up for those shoes and purse. If you are what he wants he will put in the work to win you over. It may not always be with flowers and cards, flowers die, and cards can easily get lost. I am talking about his time, talent and effort. I am not trying to paint a picture of a weak man; this canvas beholds the picture of a man that is sure in what he so desires. If he is completely honest with himself and you, he will let you know that by date three he already knows what his plans are for you. You just have to pay

How Will You Be Listed?

attention. If he is who you want guess what? The same applies. You will do the things that are necessary to love and honor him the way in which he deserves to be loved and honored. Good men are hard to come by so if you have done so you better hold on to what you have. Somebody will be glad to release you of the headache you are claiming that he is, somebody will be glad for the headache.

How Will You Be Listed?

How Will You Be Listed?

NEVER MARRY THE MOMENT

This topic of discussion is a big one. Some good moments can occur while dating or even seeing a man. There are times when the moment will feel just right, the stars are shining bright and the moon is as full as it could ever be. He is saying all the right things and honey…… you know the rest. But you better seek God and see if this is just a MOMENT! Y'all may seem like the ideal couple and everyone around may agree but, you better seek God! Yes, the sex can be the best you ever had but it wont last til death do you part. You better know that is who God has set aside for you. You may wonder why I

How Will You Be Listed?

am saying this. Well, here is the thing sis, Marriage is work and if you don't have the will to work for it then it will not work for you. In the tough times the only thing that is gonna keep you grounded and at home is GENUINE LOVE! See, that moment that we were talking of earlier will one day die. If y'all are meant for each other then plenty other moments will occur and they will all get sweeter with time. As much as I hate to say it, the truth of the matter remains. Life will happen. No, it does not have to be infidelity it doesn't even have to be lies. It can be something as simple as what type seasonings will y'all agree to use or what type broom to sweep with. Yep, something just that simple can cause you to spiral off into a big argument. Sounds simple but sis, trust me. That thing can pop off and cause you to pop off right along with it. I know! You may say,

How Will You Be Listed?

I know my man better than that. To you I say, OKAY THEN!

 In the moment everything is just right, money, dreams, aspirations, goals. Yep, all of it. Then after that moment passes you will wonder who you were sharing all of that with. Yep, that is when you gotta know that I not only love him, but God ordained us to be together. See, if the enemy can stop y'all at the small stuff you will never graduate to the big stuff because you will walk away from it all and won't even care if its right or wrong to do so. A lot of people allow the moment to get them into a lifelong commitment with someone that they can't imagine themselves away from. I am not saying that marriage is all bad, please do not think that this is what I am saying. I love being married; I am forever grateful to be. I am even more grateful that I did not marry because the moment seemed

How Will You Be Listed?

right. Yes, I have had quite a few moments that seemed right, but they were not. I am not ashamed to say this because IF you listen it's gonna help you. But if you are a "Know it all" this is only good for sweeping up trash or taking up space on your device. I see it like driving a car. Before you leave the house, you need to know that gas is in your car, air is in your tires and these days and times make sure your phone is charged and you have your mask and hand sanitizer! Just because air is in your tires does not mean that the air will not seep out on the way. The tank maybe full of gas but by the time you get where you are going the tank could be empty but just because the air seeps out of the tire and the gas runs out the tank does not mean you get rid of the car, no! You refill the tire and you refill the tank because you value the car. See, you realize that you need that car to get to where you need to be and if it is the car that

How Will You Be Listed?

you are going to continue to drive you have to put in the necessary work that keeps you driving safely and properly. I hope all that made sense to you. If it didn't READ IT AGAIN. LOL!

How Will You Be Listed?

How Will You Be Listed?

JESUS HAS TO BE YOUR FOUNDATION

Unless I am building a house with the intentions of it falling, I had better build that house on a SURE FOUNDATION. I better not be foolish and build a mansion on the ocean. The house is pretty, and the ocean is relaxing but I cannot establish a sure foundation on top of the water. The same is so in a union. Jesus has to be the foundation. Am I saying you have to pray in your Heavenly language every second, No! However, know that Jesus needs to be the basis on which your marriage exists. He needs to be the glue that is keeping you together. Not your bestie nor your work family. Yes, they will all be in attendance on your wedding day they just won't be going

How Will You Be Listed?

home with you. Their advice maybe good but you need to know if it's Godly advice. When Jesus is your foundation then you will pray before making any decisions, you won't go to bed mad because Jesus is not the author of confusion. You won't call up your cousins and discuss your husband's weaknesses you will simply go up in prayer. When we build on Jesus, we can be assured that the structure will last, and it will be sure! It is in Him that we LIVE, MOVE AND HAVE OUR BEING. This applies to your marriage also. When the bills come in, gather them together and pray over them even if you have the money in the bank. Maybe you were wrongfully charged, and your prayer will draw conviction and cause you to be eligible for a refund, don't leave God out! This maybe your first-time cooking, pray! Believe that He will hear your plea. Always come together and pray. God answers prayer. Prayer is not

How Will You Be Listed?

only you and your husband telling God the way you both feel. It is also waiting and listening to see what God has to say. When you pray wait around to see what instructions are given. Pray in faith, believing that God is surely able to do exceeding, abundantly above all you could ever ask or imagine. There is a story in the Bible that talks about the importance of building a house on a sure foundation.

Matthew 7:24-27 New International Version (NIV)

The Wise and Foolish Builders

24 "Therefore everyone who hears these words of mine and puts them into practice is like a wise man who built his house on the rock. 25 The rain came down, the streams rose, and the winds blew and beat against that house; yet it did not fall, because it had its

How Will You Be Listed?

foundation on the rock. 26 But everyone who hears these words of mine and does not put them into practice is like a foolish man who built his house on sand. 27 The rain came down, the streams rose, and the winds blew and beat against that house, and it fell with a great crash."

As practical as this may seem, it is real, and it can pertain to every area of our lives. We must do things God's way if we expect His blessings and results. Yes, it takes time to build God's way and it can be disheartening to see folk completing before us that started after us but, is the foundation sure? There is a difference in swelling and growth. Swelling, though it mimics growth could have an underlying infection that is causing the change in size. Whereas growth is complete and full from the inside out. No seed planted today begins blooming tonight.

How Will You Be Listed?

It takes time. You may say you don't have time well all you have done this far is wait if we wanna be honest about it. So, why not wait with the provisions of God? He has a plan as a matter of fact it is written in Jeremiah 29:11-13. 11 For I know the plans I have for you," declares the Lord, "plans to prosper you and not to harm you, plans to give you hope and a future. 12 Then you will call on me and come and pray to me, and I will listen to you. 13 You will seek me and find me when you seek me with all your heart.

 You will never find a better one to trust with your future than Jesus. He has the blueprint the question is do you have the time?

How Will You Be Listed?

How Will You Be Listed?

Tell someone about this book.

Conclusion

In my close I would like to say:

You are BEAUTIFUL you are God's great gift to man. Any man in his right mind has to honor you. He must see the Blessing that you are. If by chance this is not the case, simply see it as God's way of saying NOT YET! Guess what? That in and of itself is a Blessing. I know for myself rejection doesn't feel like a blessing but I can assure you that every area of my life that I have been rejected in has in one way or another brought me blessings that I am not able to even put into words. Give God time to work and in doing so let Him work on you, prepare you, fill your life with JOY. Heal you from past hurts, pain, and rejection. I am excited for you and I am glad that you have read this, I know that it

How Will You Be Listed?

will make a difference in your life in the best way possible because I did not tell myself to write this. Truth is I did not even want to do this because it causes me a measure of exposure and transparency that I was not ready for but whatever it takes to help my sister overcome, HERE I AM! Do not allow the virus of hate and hurt to infest your soul another day. The abuse happened, the pain happened, the divorce happened, the molestation happened, the infidelity happened, the betrayal happened, the rape happened, the neglect happened! Yes, all of that happened. There is no way of denying this! You have to know that none of it happened TO YOU instead it happened FOR YOU! It happened so that God could position you in the very spot that you are in right now. See, God does all things well and He knows exactly what He is doing, it all had to happen and one day you are going to rejoice at the

How Will You Be Listed?

fact that it did. Especially when you see it as the road to lead you to a BETTER YOU!

It is to God ALONE that I give All Glory!
I am excited for you!

How Will You Be Listed?

Follow me on Facebook
The Birthing Chamber
Unlocked

How Will You Be Listed?

My Dearest Sis,

First and foremost, THANK YOU for entrusting me to come into your space and share with you a part of my heart. I appreciate this more than you will ever know! Your support means so much to me.

Secondly, be encouraged! I did not write this to beat up on you. My intent was not at all one of badgering you. But these are some life lessons that I have learned along the way and I want to see you BETTER! I believe that we do a very good job of discrediting one another and the time has now arrived that WE stand unified. TOGETHER WE WIN! If I can help you through my life experiences, I will! If you can help another female through your life experiences, you should! I am in no way proclaiming to be an expert of any sort, I am yet learning. However, I am skilled in what I

How Will You Be Listed?

do know. Nobody can take away the life experiences that I have had. I consider those experiences to be equivalent to a degree of some sort. I am just talking about the ones that pertain to self-worth here, I have a plenty others that I will discuss with you in another book……. (I keep saying this hmmm.) They are mine, I went through them, I endured the pain, I beheld the embarrassment, I dealt with the shame and I made it out! I did not just make it out, I made it out ALIVE. The mere fact that I made it out alive lets me know that I am to make it medicine for someone else. Not just someone but YOU! All too often we mask and hide or put away the pain associated with going through when this is the antidote for someone else's virus. You have the antibodies within you to help some other woman from suffering the viruses of LIFE! So, read it and take every word in, use the note sheets provided to write out YOUR

How Will You Be Listed?

story. God Bless and I will see you in our next
SESSION! Together, we are BETTER!

Sincerely,
 Evangelist
Jennifer Johnson Cook, Author

ABOUT THE AUTHOR

Evangelist Jennifer Johnson Cook

is the daughter of Mr. Isaac and the late "Mrs. Ruby W. Johnson. Born and raised in Bishopville, SC. She is a 1996 graduate of Bishopville High School as well as a 2011 graduate of Kenneth Shuler School of Cosmetology, Columbia SC as a Licensed Cosmetologist and a 2012 graduate of this school as a Licensed Cosmetology Instructor.   Jennifer is DELIGHTFULLY married to Mr. Rodney R. Cook and with God's help they parent three adorable children, Rodneya, Janiyah and Jeremiah

Jennifer accepted her call into ministry in 2003 and has been fulfilling "THE CALL" ever since! Jennifer and her husband are humbled to partner in ministry by way of Stage plays and short skits with God's grace and guidance, the most recent one was, "Come to the Light" May 2017. She has also starred in a movie addressing domestic violence and child abuse entitled, "Escape to Tell."

How Will You Be Listed?

Be it through the Word of song,
Evangelizing, Prayer, Stage plays, skits,
styling hair, or by the words of a newly
written book, Jennifer firmly believes that
Jesus is not to be confined by the four walls
of the local Church. She believes that the
WORLD is her parish, and with God's help
she will spread the Word to all mankind!

How Will You Be Listed?

Pure Thoughts Publishing LLC